The Hunting & Fishing For Survival Handbook

By: Tristan Trouble

Published in USA by:

CDI Publications, LLC
P.O BOX #9
Boynton Beach
FL 33425

© Copyright 2018

ISBN-13: 978-1717008244
ISBN-10: 1717008240

Table of Contents

Introduction

While many people hunt and fish for sport, and/or to supplement the food they have for the year, these skills sets will become extremely important to survival should a disaster occur. In addition to foraging for wild edibles, preppers may need to hunt and fish in order to survive if/when disaster strikes.

In this guide book we are going to cover several topics of interest for both hunting and fishing. We will discuss various methods of fishing, some conventional others unconventional. The same will apply to the hunting section of this guide book when we get to it; the conventional will discuss the use of modern weapons and firearms, whereas the unconventional will discuss skills such as trapping, snaring, etc.

Readers will be given detailed information on how to perform various fishing techniques, such as noodling for catfish, how to spearfish with a conventional spear as well as a homemade version, as well as how to net and trap fish. Several types of angling skills will also be covered, such as handlining, trotlining, and jigging, which will be accompanied by a variety of rod fishing techniques like bait casting, bank fishing, fly fishing and ice fishing, just to name a few.

On the hunting side of things, topics will include discussions on bowhunting, the use of firearms for hunting, the use of bait piles and decoys, lures, scents, and animal calls, as well as how to track and trap a variety of small game animals.

Although brief, additional methods of obtaining food are also discussed in this book, such as establishing a garden, with various configurations detailed for the reader, as well as how to purchase surplus food from emergency preparedness distributors and stockpile it for the future.

This guide book will finish off by discussing various means of cooking food in an off grid situation. This section will focus on the unconventional methods of cooking food and will include the use of campfires, underground ovens, and sun ovens, as well as a handful of other techniques that may be handy in a pinch.

If you are interested in prepping or spend a fair amount of time in the great outdoors, then these are skills you will want to have available should you ever need them. It is far better to be prepared for a disaster and never need to use the skills than it is to be faced with surviving a disaster and have no skills, gear, or means of making it through safely.

This guide book contains information that has been included for educational purposes, but which may provide benefits to novice emergency preppers and seasoned outdoor enthusiasts alike. These skill sets require ample practice before they can be mastered. If/where possible, seek a local guide to assist you with learning these skills for the region you reside in; there are several variables that are regional which are best addressed by a local sportsman/woman.

Aquatic Foraging

We start this guide book out with a discussion on aquatic foraging and fishing. Individuals who live near the coast may have the advantage of aquatic foraging. Aquatic foraging consists of searching for and securing such items as seaweed, crabs, clams, and shellfish that can be found in close proximity to the seashore.

Searching for Seaweed

Individuals who live along the coast may have the advantage of being able to locate dense forests of healthy, edible seaweed. Seaweed forests thrive just off shore and represent a vast source of wild food that remains largely untapped here in the United States, which is amazing considering that several other cultures around the world forage for and use seaweed as a staple in their traditional diet.

When it comes to seaweed, they are separated and categorized according to color; red, brown, and green. Although seaweed may appear to grow in abundance, like any other food group in the wild edible category, this must be harvested sustainably; remember that there is an entire ecosystem dependent on this underwater vegetation, so only take what you can use within a given day and return for more later, if need be.

Harvesting seaweed consists of removing the top third of an individual plant, using a very sharp knife or set of scissors. The remainder of the plant is left intact and attached to the rock it calls home. Seaweed has no roots. It attaches to rocks by what is referred to as a holdfast, which acts somewhat like a root system but not entirely.

Seaweed, like other wild plant species, has edible varieties as well as poisonous varieties. This means that you need to have the ability to properly identify what you are about to harvest; the universal edibility test is not recommended for use with seaweed varieties. It is highly recommended that you locate a seaweed foraging class, mentor, or detailed guidebook with color pictures and definitions, before embarking on a seaweed harvesting excursion.

If you come across an unknown species of seaweed, leave it be. It is far too risky to harvest from an unverified source. Speaking of risky harvesting practices, avoid gathering seaweed that has washed up on shore. Seaweed that has washed ashore has usually started to decompose, which will cause it to taste horrible and smell bad to boot.

Always practice safety when out searching for seaweed. The best times to venture out in search of edible seaweed is when the tide is out. Seaweed tends to lurk just beyond the low tide table, so waiting until the tide goes out makes it easier to harvest seaweed in a shallow water situation. Remember, there will be slippery sharp rocks to traverse, so sheath your knife/scissors when moving about and try to avoid any personal injury.

Consuming Seaweed

Seaweeds can be consumed in a variety of ways. Some species can be harvested, washed, rinsed, and added to a meal, such as a salad without needing any further processing. Other species of seaweed are best eaten when they've been dehydrated and ground into a powder, such as a seasoning. Some varieties can also be chopped down and added to stews/soups, etc. All seaweed species can be dried and beaten into a powder, then used as a flavor substitute/enhancer. Several varieties can be harvested and allowed to dry into a jerky-like edible.

There have been several books written on the subject of seaweed preparation and recipes; we highly recommend finding one that deals with the local area as they will have recipes for the types of seaweed generally found along the coastal areas where you reside. Most seaweed varieties can be boiled and eaten, and the broth can then be consumed or allowed to gel, which can then be added to different dessert items. Seaweeds have also been used as flavor enhancing agents when food is steamed, such as a clambake, or luau pit.

Medicinal Uses

The majority of iodine we find on pharmacy shelves is harvested from one of two sources; red or brown algae. Iodine is an important component for supporting a healthy functioning thyroid gland. Several seaweeds also contain a substantial amount of potassium chloride which can be used as a salt substitute. If used as a broth and allowed to cool into a gel, the gel material can be used as an ingredient for burn and bruise remedies, as well as hand lotions.

Common Seaweed Edibles

- **Kelp** - comes from the brown algae category and is the most commonly consumed variety of seaweed.
    - ✓ Wakame—is a member of the kelp family and is a protein and calcium rich food source. It is most often used in salads and stews.
    - ✓ Kombu—another member of the kelp family that is a rich source of calcium, iodine, iron, magnesium, protein,

phosphorous, sodium and potassium, as well as vitamins A, C, D, E, K.

✓ Arame—yet another member of the kelp family and a very rich source of iodine and iron.

➤ **Nori** - this is the seaweed you see wrapped around sushi. If you're new to eating seaweed, this is probably where you should start as this variety has a sweet, yet slightly meaty flavor. It is a rich source of protein, the richest of all seaweed varieties. It also contains a high concentration of calcium, iron, copper, iodine, zinc, and potassium as well as a handful of vitamins.

➤ **Dulse** - this seaweed comes from the red algae category and is also known as sea lettuce. It is considered a good source of dietary fiber, calcium, protein, magnesium, and iodine, as well as vitamins A, B6, B12, C, E.

Searching for Shellfish

Before you begin foraging for shellfish you need to be aware of where to search for them and when, as well as how to prepare them once you've harvested them; it serves no purpose to forage shellfish and not know how to cook them prior to eating them. Like many other plants and animals, there is a season for finding fresh shellfish, and there are certain places to avoid when looking for fresh shellfish. First and foremost, all shellfish will fall into one of two categories; mollusks or crustaceans.

- Mollusks are invertebrates which means they have soft bodies that are not segmented; most shellfish that fall into this category also have a calcium rich outer shell. Mollusks can be searched for and harvested.
- Crustaceans are arthropods which means they have a calcium rich outer shell that protects a soft body which is segmented. Crustaceans also have appendages and often display multiple sets of antennae. Crustaceans must be hunted rather than foraged.

The mollusks that most people forage for considered "filter feeders." This basically means they constantly and consistently filter the water around them through their soft bodies, extracting any nutrients that are present. Sadly, this also means that they can extract and retain potentially harmful toxins that might also be present in the water. With that in mind, it is highly recommended that shellfish only be harvested from coastal regions where sewage, toxic chemical spills, oil spills, etc., are not a concern. If the area has ever experienced one of these events, avoid harvesting in that location.

You should also refrain from harvesting shellfish that are located in enclosed areas of water, or in places where waterways are narrowed, such as harbors, marinas, boat docks, as well as rivers, streams, and creeks that may flow into the ocean from further inland.

At certain times of the year, coastal regions may also experience "algae blooms," often referred to as "red tides," which can result in the poisoning of shellfish in the immediate vicinity. Algae blooms often occur during the warmer months; however, this isn't always the case, there are exceptions to the rule. In the northern hemisphere algae blooms are most likely to occur during late spring and throughout the summer when temperatures are warmest.

When algae bloom does occur, they are usually

reported by local news agencies who receive firsthand information from regional port authorities, as well as warnings from local environmental protection agencies.

If/when these warnings are issued, they are often accompanied by a local ban on foraging for shellfish, especially if there is a health concern. Stay informed of these events during the shellfish foraging season and heed any warnings issues; consuming toxic shellfish can result in fatality.

In addition to possible shellfish poisoning, you also need to be aware that shellfish foraging is often a seasonal event. Local authorities determine when the season opens and closes as well as what, if any, restrictions will be in place and enforced. These restrictions may be broad spectrum, which means they will include several forms of shellfish, or they may be more specific and target a certain shellfish species within the region. Violating these restrictions, and/or harvesting out of season, can result in criminal charges, fines, and loss of foraging privileges.

Mentionable Mollusks

The mollusks mentioned here are those that are the easiest to forage for and harvest. These are also the most recognizable to find and they are all considered sustainable resources that can be found without the need for special traps or hunting equipment. In most cases you can simply pick them up and place them in a holding container; however, in some cases you may need a knife to pry them from their home.

- ➢ **Mussels** - are the most sought after shellfish in the mollusk category. They are among the easiest shellfish to forage and harvest. When low tide arrives, they become exposed and can be found attached to rocky outcrops, sand bars, etc. You seldom have to dig for mussels, you simply need a container to carry them in. When foraging for mussels, make sure their shells are tightly shut and that they smell and appear to be fresh. If you come across a mussel with a slightly open shell, try to pinch it closed; if the mussel is still alive then it will react by slamming its shell shut tightly. If the mussel is no longer alive the shell will remain ajar. Discard any mussels with shells that remain ajar or that are broken.
- ➢ **Clams & Cockles** - are also relatively easy to forage and harvest. These two species of shellfish prefer to bury themselves in the sand as the tide is going out. When the tide starts to come back in, small breather

holes begin appearing in the sand as these shellfish prepare to embrace the waters of the rising tides. The same precautions for mussels should also be applied to harvesting clams and cockles with regards to shells that remain open or broken.

➤ **Oysters** - these shellfish tend to reside just beyond the waterline for low tide and prefer the nutrient dense waters that are often found in tidal marshes. They can also be found on sand bars, attached to rock outcrops, jetties, and harbor walls. The same precautions apply to oysters as to the shellfish mentioned above, especially with regards to shells that are ajar or broken.

Crustaceans for Consideration

When it comes to crustaceans, you will more than likely need to set "pots," which are basically traps, in order to catch enough of them to make a meal. Shrimp, crab, lobster, and crawdads (crayfish) are the most commonly sought after members of the crustacean category.

➤ **Shrimp** - there are several species of shrimp that can be harvested; some of them from shallow waters, others from depths of 4,500 feet or more. Some species can be found in shallow water environments, such as tidal pools and sea walls.

➤ **Crabs** - there are also several species of crab that can be harvested close to shore, however, the most sought after specimens are normally trawled for in deep cold water regions, such as the Bering Sea that borders Alaska. Crab species that can be harvested close to shore will more than likely be found hiding in the holes and crevices created by a rock wall.

➤ **Lobsters** - these crustaceans are normally caught off shore in lobster pots that are dropped to the ocean floor in deep water off shore. While some can be located in water no more than 15' deep, most are found at depths of 1,000 feet or more.

Fishing for Survival

Fishing for survival can encompass many forms of fishing. In this segment we will discuss several of those options; some will be conventional, and others will not. While fishing gear is often an essential piece of recommended gear for preppers and outdoor enthusiasts, it isn't always something we carry with us on a regular basis. It is for this purpose that we cover the unconventional methods of fishing to ensure that you are aware of them and are able to use them to survive an otherwise dire situation.

Noodling for Catfish

While this might seem like a new method of fishing, it has been around for quite some time. In fact, noodling can trace its roots all the way back to early Native Americans who are thought to be the first humans to master this fishing technique.

Noodling is considered illegal in all but 13 states in the US; however, catching catfish with a baited hook is considered legal in all 50 states. This is because some experts think that noodling places the catfish population at risk. Most states have some form of catfish conservation efforts in place to track and record the rise and fall of regional catfish populations. Even in states that allow noodling, there are often restrictions on the number of catfish that can be caught and kept. This is because noodling is done during the spawn when male cats are guarding the eggs of the next generation, so grabbing a catfish during this time exposes the eggs to vulnerabilities and places the entire population at risk.

Step 1

Noodling takes place during the spawn, which occurs during the spring and fall when water temperatures rise to an average of 70°F. The biggest male catfish will guard the area where eggs are present, normally in underwater hiding places, such as toppled trees, sunken logs, beneath big rocks, or in crevices created by rock walls, under boat docks, etc. These hiding places are almost always in shallow water where the temperatures tend to remain relatively warmer than in deeper water.

Step 2

For safety reasons, noodling should always consist of at least 2 adults, and the bigger the adults the better. It is not unheard of for catfish to grow large enough to dwarf a full grown man. Catfish are also known to be aggressive; it is not uncommon for large aggressive catfish to pull children and small adults underwater during noodling excursions, so you need to have someone around who can help pull you back to the surface should a catfish take you under. This is also the reason that noodling should only be done in shallow water where you can stand up and breach the surface without much trouble.

Step 3

Once you locate a potential hiding place, you need to block off all exits except the hole you will be using as an entrance. This can be done with rocks big enough to block the hole, sandbags if you want to lug them around, or whatever you can arrange in makeshift fashion to achieve the desired result. The best approach to blocking off the exits is to use other people/noodlers as this will maximize your chances of successfully landing a catfish.

Step 4

Inspection of the hiding place comes next. You should also apply safety precautions during this step; catfish are not the only creatures that may be hiding in the hole you have chosen. For inspection purposes you may want to use a stick, or at the very least a wire mesh glove covered hand. Snapping turtles, venomous snakes, and even beavers could be encountered during the inspection process. If inspection reveals, or leads one to believe, that any of these animals are in the hiding hole, then make a slow, safe retreat and search elsewhere.

Step 5

If the inspection reveals that a large catfish is present, then it's time to get wet. Your feet should be firmly planted approximately shoulder width apart. When you're sure of your footing, it's time to shove your dominant hand down into the hole. The object of noodling is to elicit an aggressive response from the catfish who is protecting the eggs; you want the fish to bite down on your hand. If you do not receive an aggressive response you may have to agitate the fish to provoke it into action.

Step 6

Additional precautions to be aware of and employ when noodling include, but are not limited to;

- ➢ Avoid deep water
- ➢ Avoid areas with strong currents
- ➢ Be aware of barbs along the pectoral fin; very sharp and can cut into flesh

> ➢ The largest catfish ever caught weighed in at 646 lbs.
> ➢ Several catfish species weigh more than 50 lbs. on average
> ➢ A large aggressive catfish can thrash hard enough to knock the wind out of an adult human, and/or break a few ribs
> ➢ Noodling should only be done with an experienced guide, especially if you've never done it before

Spearfishing for Survival

Spearfishing is another ancient fishing method that several civilizations throughout history have used to provide food for sustenance. After various hand fishing techniques, spearfishing is probably the next oldest method known to man.

Conventional Spearfishing

Modern day spearfishing techniques have evolved quite nicely. Those who participate in spearfishing today, have the advantage of being able to use spearguns that employ compressed gas, as well as modern diving equipment which includes snorkeling and scuba diving gear. That being said, there are several countries where spearfishing with scuba gear is deemed illegal, as is the use of mechanically assisted spearguns.

Modern spearfishing can also include the use of elastic assisted spears, also referred to as "trigger-less," or "pole" spears; they may also be referred to as "Hawaiian slings." For the most part, spearfishing is conducted in shallow water in depths up to 131 feet and can be done in both freshwater and saltwater environments.

If you're interested in modern spearfishing you will need some special gear and you will need to locate and hire an experienced guide; this is not an adventure that the novice should attempt alone. Spearfishing should always employ safety and consist of two or more participants, one of which should have years of experience. You will also need some special gear:

- ➢ **Speargun** - a piece of equipment specifically designed to fire a single spear at a target fish
- ➢ **Pole spear** - also referred to as hand spears; essentially a handheld spear that encompasses an elastic band opposite the pointed end of the shaft which is used to propel the spear through the water
- ➢ **Hawaiian sling** - similar to a pole spear, but incorporates a tube through which the spear is fired
- ➢ **Wetsuit** - there are several types and styles of wetsuits; some are even made specifically for spearfishing
- ➢ **Weight Vest/Belt** - this equipment assists the diver with descending to the desired depth. Most of this equipment has been designed with "quick release" features that allow the diver to drop the gear should they need to ascend quickly
- ➢ **Swimming Fins** - this equipment also comes in a wide variety of styles, shapes, and configurations;

some are even designed for specific types of spearfishing (free-diving and scuba)

➢ **Scuba Knife** - must be sharp and carried at all times. The knife can be used to cut the diver free should they become tangled in a line. It can also be used finish a kill and keep a fish from thrashing about (an act which might draw the attention of sharks)

➢ **Buoy & Dive Flag** - this equipment is deployed to alert other boaters passing by that a diver is in the area.

➢ **Floatline** - this is essentially a "lifeline" of sorts and connects the diver to the buoy by way of the weight belt. This helps prevent the diver from being carried away by underwater currents

➢ **Protective Gloves** - should provide thermal protection when diving in colder water or to deeper depths. Should also provide a layer of protection against the spines and teeth of a thrashing fish who has been shot with a spear

➢ **Stringer** - used to secure fish that have been speared.

➢ **Snorkel & Diving Mask** - this equipment should be designed specifically for the sport of spearfishing

➢ **Scuba Gear** - this equipment may or may not be designed specifically for spearfishing

Unconventional Spearfishing

Unconventional spearfishing involves the use of homemade equipment. This is the type of spearfishing that will more than likely be employed by preppers in an otherwise dire situation. This is the method that several early civilizations used to supplement food sources and ensure their survival.

In basic terms, it consists of fabricating a spear from natural material, such as a bamboo shoot, tree branch, etc. One end of the raw material is whittled into a sharp point; it may even be split into 2-3 points, then banded together to create a trident of sorts; also referred to as a "gig," or "gigging rig." The person fishing then patrols the shoreline from land, or by boat, in search of fish swimming in shallow water. When a fish is located the spear is jabbed into the water in hopes of puncturing the fish, or at the very least, pinning it to the bed of the lake, river, stream, or creek.

When using this method to spearfish, the person fishing must make adjustments to account for refraction on the surface of the water; fish will appear to be resting at a slightly higher elevation in the fisher's line of sight than they actually are. Compensation for this refraction is accomplished by aiming an inch or two lower than where the fish appears to be; this becomes easier to achieve with experience.

Spearfishing in freshwater environments is often restricted to specific species of fish and may also incorporate specific seasons for spearfishing certain types of fish. In addition to spearfishing from shore, these gigging rigs can also be used to harvest frogs and small game if the user has the experience.

In all instances of spearfishing, water clarity is probably the most important factor to take into consideration; if you cannot see the bottom of the environment you are fishing, then the water is either too deep, or it is too cloudy, both of which will have a negative impact on your success rate. While gigging from shore doesn't necessarily require employing the same safety as underwater spearfishing, novice enthusiasts should seek the assistance of an experienced guide to improve their chances of success.

Netting & Trapping Fish for Survival

The use of nets and traps is another fishing technique that has a long history of providing various civilizations with the ability to supplement food and make survival easier to achieve. Conventional fishing nets are manufactured in several configurations; however, they all embody very similar meshed features, which is the knotting of the thread used to create the net/trap itself.

Conventional fishing nets usually fall into one of two categories; shore operated, or boat operated. For the purpose of this book, we will refrain from discussing the boat operated variety as it is assumed most prepper will not be using boats during a disaster situation. When it comes to shore operated fishing nets there are two categories; conventional and unconventional. The conventional end of the spectrum consists of modern fishing equipment supplied by a manufacturer, whereas the unconventional end of the spectrum consists of fabricating a net out of raw material.

Conventional Fishing Nets & Traps

The fishing nets featured in this segment can be purchased from a distributor. There are a few options in this category which preppers may want to consider including in their gear as it will make surviving a disaster a bit easier to accomplish. Here is a short list of the conventional shore operated fishing nets that are used around the world;

> **Cast Nets** - also referred to as "throw nets," these fishing devices are round nets that are weighted evenly along the outer edge. The net is cast out over a shallow area of water where it sinks to the floor. Once the net has descended to the floor, it is hauled back in, dragging the weights along the bottom and trapping any fish caught inside. These devices have been in use for several thousand years by coastal civilizations around the world

> **Gill Nets** - these are anchored nets that are positioned along high traffic areas of a body of water, such as the mouth of a river, and normally in shallow water environments that allow the net to stretch from the surface all the way to the bed. Fish are trapped by the gills when they attempt to pass through the net. The size of the holes in the meshing of the net will determine the size of fish that can be caught using this type of device; if the holes are too large for the regional species, then the fish will flow back and forth through the net freely. If the holes are too small, the fish will not be able to pass through at all, which will also result in an unsuccessful attempt

> **Hand Nets** - also referred to as "scoop nets," these are the nets most of us are familiar with. They are generally small nets that have the outer edge attached to a hoop which is also attached to a pole. Depending on the size, these nets can be used to secure baitfish to be used for catching larger predatory species, or they can be used to dip into

schools of fish and retrieve several at a time. Fishing with these types of nets is best accomplished when a fish species is spawning, as this is the time they will travel in abundant groups. For instance, when Salmon or Smelt spawn, they normally travel upstream in a river system; this type of net will allow you to catch as many fish as you need to provide a healthy feast

This rounds out the conventional fishing nets that will be useful by all preppers during a disaster situation. There are several other conventional fishing nets available, but without a boat they are basically useless for the purpose of survival.

Conventional fishing traps are generally too big, bulky, and heavy to be included in emergency preparedness kits. It is for this reason that we refrain from discussing the use of these options. Suffice to say that if you live near a fishing village, conventional fishing traps will more than likely be available should a disaster strike.

Unconventional Fishing Nets & Traps

Unconventional fishing nets would be those created out of raw material found in the wilderness. The process of fabricating a fishing net out of raw materials would be more time consuming and trouble than building a much smaller fishing trap or basket. We will therefore focus on discussions regarding DIY fish traps that can be used during a disaster situation.

- ➤ **DIY Fishing Weirs** - like the one in the image above, can be built using sticks, stones, or whatever raw material is available. The main objective here is to channel the fish into a controllable environment where they will be easier to harvest. In the image above, the fish swim through the narrow openings into the larger pools. When there is a sufficient number of fish in the pool area, the narrow opening can be closed off temporarily with more raw material. The fish are then harvested, and the narrow entries are reopened

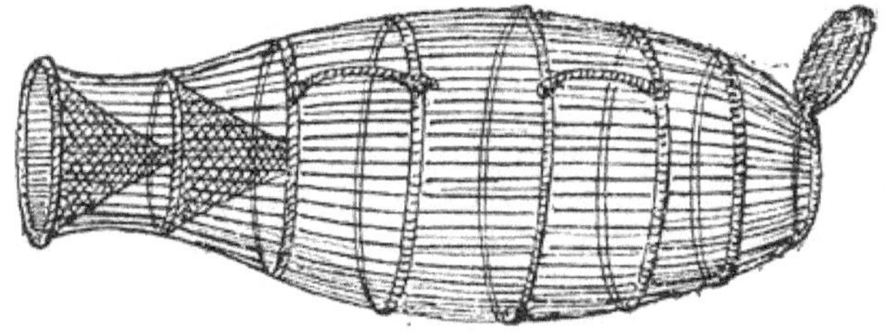

> **Woven Fish Traps** - are fishing devices that are made from raw materials found in nature. While there are several designs to choose from, the basic concepts are all the same. The trap consists of a narrow, funneled opening through which the fish swim into the main body of the trap. The main body of the trap is large enough to hold several fish and has slightly larger covered exit that can be easily opened to retrieve the fish from the trap

> ✓ A similar fishing trap can be constructed from a 2-liter bottle by simply removing the top end of the bottle, inverting it, and placing it back inside the bottle, and sealing it to the bottle body. This creates the same type of funneling system as a woven fish trap; however, retrieval of the fish from the trap often results in the destruction of the trap itself.

This completes the unconventional fishing nets and traps that will be useful in a survival situation. While there may be other ideas available from various resources, these two ideas are considered the easiest to build and use effectively.

Fish traps should be set in a shallow water environment where they will be easy to retrieve. Depending on the environment, you may also want to weigh the fish trap down to the bed with a couple strategically placed rocks. If possible, the use of bait will improve the odds catching fish successfully.

Angling

Angling is a term often used to describe fishing in general; however, the true definition of the word reveals that it pertains to a method of fishing that utilizes an "angle," or in more relatable terms, a hook. The hook is normally tied off to a fishing line and is used to secure the bait. The line holding the hook is often weighted down to help it descend to lower depths where bigger fish may be present. In some cases, the line may also hold a bobber which serves the purpose of suspending the bait at a specified depth and notifying the angler when a fish has taken the bait.

While it is possible to use the "hook, line, and sinker" configuration to handline for fish, this method often incorporates the use of a rod and reel combination that allows the angler to have greater control over placement of the hook and bait, as well as better ability to retrieve fish when they have taken the bait. When it comes to using angling as a method of fishing for survival, there are several options to become familiar with. The ideas shared in this section will cover the angling techniques considered to be suitable for use in a disaster situation; many of these same techniques can be used for everyday fishing as well. Angling can be divided into three separate categories; line fishing, rod and reel fishing, and unconventional fishing.

Line Fishing

Line fishing is exactly what the name implies; the use of line to catch fish. There are several ways that line fishing can be accomplished. Success will largely depend on experience and the environment where these methods are being tried.

- ✓ **Droplines** - are very similar to trotlines; however, they run vertically in a body of water rather than horizontally. A dropline consists of a single strand of fishing line that is weighted at one end and outfitted with a float on the other. Several hooks are tied to the fishing line at various intervals. These hooks are then baited, and the weighted end of the line is dropped into the water; the flotation end of the line should remain on the surface of the body of water. The dropline is allowed to remain in the water for several hours and is checked periodically to retrieve any fish caught. The bait is then refreshed, and the line placed back in the water in the same location or a different one

✓ **Handlines** - are basically fishing rigs that do not incorporate the use of a rod and reel. One end of the line contains the hook, bait, and sinker and the other end of the line remains wrapped around the dominant hand of the fisher, a stick, or other retrieval device. The baited hook and line are cast into a body of water and fishing commences as it would with a conventional rod and reel combination. When a fish bites on the baited hook, the angler must retrieve the line by pulling the fish to shore while simultaneously wrapping excess line around the dominant hand. Once the fish has been removed the bait can be replaced and the fishing can continue

✓ **Jigging** - this type of fishing consists of using a line that is baited with a soft bodied lure that is molded around a weighted hook, also referred to as a jig. The jig is cast into the water and retrieved slowly; this creates a jerking action that causes the jig to "bounce" off the bottom of the environment, mimicking the vertical up and down actions of a disabled fish

✓ **Trotlining** - very similar to droplining. The biggest difference is that a trotline is suspended horizontally across a body of water. The mainline can be positioned above or below the surface of the water.

Trotlines are usually set across rivers, streams, and creeks, where each end of the main line can be tied off to an existing structure such as a tree. Branch lines are attached to the main line at various intervals and at different lengths. The hooks of the branch lines are baited and once the trotline has been set, the branch lines dangle freely in the water. Trotlines are then checked periodically, at which time fish are retrieved and baits are reset

Rod & Reel Fishing

Rod & Reel Fishing is also exactly as the name implies. In order to fish using these methods you will need a rod and reel, link, hooks, bait, lures, sinkers, and floats. Through the use of this gear and specialized equipment, the

individual fishing experiences greater control over the fishing line. The rod allows the fisher to cast the bait further and with better accuracy to the area desired. The reel makes retrieval of the line much easier to accomplish than traditional handlining.

- ➢ **Shore Fishing** - refers to fishing from the shore of a lake or the banks of a river, stream, or creek. Fishing from shore may seem a bit more restrictive than fishing from a boat; however, with the right equipment and experience, successful fishing can be achieved. To use this method, one simply baits the hook or rigs the line, then casts the hook into the water. Depending on what type of fishing is being done, the baited hook is either left in place for a period of time as the fisher waits for a bite, or the rigged line is cast into the water and the lure is retrieved using a fast or slow motion retrieval process
- ➢ **Bait Casting** - can be done from shore or a boat and consists of using lures rather than live bait, although live bait can be added if desired. The lure is rigged to the line and the bait is cast to the desired fishing location, then retrieved using a fast or slow motion retrieval process. This type of fishing may also include the use of a leader which makes changing lures quicker and easier to accomplish, especially in low light situations
- ➢ **Fly Fishing** - is often done in rivers and streams where the water is constantly in motion. The rod and reel combination for fly fishing is similar, yet

different than, that which is used for traditional bait casting. Fly fishing is either done from shore or from within the body of water being fished. Artificial lures in the shape of "flies," are tied off to the fishing line and cast out over a body of water using a special casting procedure. The fly is then "landed" on top of the water and allowed to drift with the current. These flies are designed to resemble natural insects that live in and around these bodies of water. The fish in the river/stream will "rise" to inspect and eat the fly, at which time the hook is set, and the fish is retrieved using the reel at the base of the rod

➢ **Ice Fishing** - consists of using handlines, drop lines, and rod and reel combinations to catch fish from an ice covered body of water, normally a lake but it is done on a few rivers that freeze over solid enough during the winter to withstand the weight of people. Anglers walk out onto the ice and drill a hole in the location they wish to fish in. They then go about arranging their fishing gear to be dropped through the hole. When a fish bites the angler retrieves the fish through the hole in the ice, rebaits the hook, and resets the line

Unconventional Fishing

Unconventional fishing techniques are those that employ equipment that isn't necessarily invented, designed, or engineered to be used for fishing. Most of these methods will not be available in a disaster situation; however, they are gaining in popularity and may serve a purpose for normal day to day fishing excursions when disaster is not a threat.

> **Drone Fishing** - is a relatively new method of fishing that has several advantages for the experienced drone operating angler. Drones can be outfitted with fishing rigs, many of which look like dropline configurations. The drones and fishing tackle are flown over a body of water. When a

school of fish is located, the drone is flown to a height that allows the fishing line and rig to be introduced to the water. The drone then hovers in place or makes small movements to "jig" the bait in an attempt to entice the fish into biting. When a fish strikes, the drone is then flown upward with a quick jerking motion to set the hook. Once the hook has been set the drone is flown back to shore where the angler can then retrieve the fish and reset the drone supported fishing rig

➤ **RC Fishing** - makes use of radio controlled boats and inventive fishing rigs. The RC boats and rigs are driven around the lake, normally with the rigged line flowing out behind the boat. When a fish strikes, the boat is driven back to shore where the angle can retrieve the fish and reset the gear

➤ **Culvert Dam Fishing** - this process consists of using something large enough to block one end of a culvert that runs beneath a road, such as those constructed for creeks and streams; a piece of plywood usually works just fine. One to two people stand on the upstream side of the road holding the plywood, while another person stands on the downstream side of the road holding a scoop net, a fishing basket, or a bucket. The anglers on the upstream side of the road then block off the entrance to the culvert creating a makeshift dam. This causes the water in the culvert to drain out of the downstream side, carrying all the fish in the culvert with it; the angler on this side of the culvert catches the fish as they fall with the draining water. Once the fish are caught the anglers on the upstream side of the road remove the plywood and allow the culvert to fill again. This process can be repeated throughout the day as long as intervals are observed between damming periods

Small Game Hunting

Hunting involves the act of killing animals. Hunting can be done for sport or to simply secure more food. Hunting can also involve trapping, tracking, and/or baiting animals, although laws regarding the use of bait vary from one state to the next. As a method of survival and sustenance, evidence suggests that hunting has been around for more than 2 million years. Even as man began domesticating animals, hunting continued to be an important component of human survival.

When it comes to hunting there are basically two

categories; small game and large game. When it comes to hunting for survival, the small game category is the one most preppers will need to focus on. Unless you are caught up in a disaster with a large group of people, chances are you'll be traveling as a smaller, tight knit group of no more than 5-6, and small game should more than suffice for your needs.

There are several advantages to small game hunting in a survival situation. It is a more sustainable practice simply because there is less to waste. Most small game animals are easier to clean and prepare, and they are much easier to transport back to base camp. Small game animals are often more abundant than large game animals; squirrels and rabbits are plentiful in the forest, whereas you may go days or weeks without seeing a large game animal at all. In addition to providing meat, small game hunting can also provide bones, sinew, fur, and hides, all of which can be used to make other items. Sinew, for example, can be used to manufacture cordage, while hides can be tanned into leather.

Those who have limited hunting experience, or who

are lacking hunting experience altogether, are advised to seek guidance from a professional hunter before embarking on a hunting excursion themselves. Preppers should become familiar with a variety of hunting methods, strategies, and equipment before venturing into the wilderness for any length of time. Readers are advised not to attempt hunting by themselves until they have gained the relevant knowledge and experience to do so, which can only come from hunting with experienced individuals and guides.

North American Small Game

Small game animals of North America can be found in several locations. For the most part game animals avoid highly congested areas such as major cities. When they are seen living in heavily populated areas they generally stick to the parks and/or areas close to a source of water; they are seldom seen roaming the same streets as people.

In suburban and rural areas, small game animals might call your backyard home; they can be found roaming through neighboring yards, trees, and gardens. The type of game animals you will encounter in these areas will depend on the surrounding environment. For instance, you won't find many squirrels running around the neighborhoods of Arizona that are surrounded by desert landscape; however, you will find several different species of them in neighborhoods that are surrounded by forests and rural countryside. The following is a list of small game animals in North America that are either hunted seasonally, or that can be hunted in a survival situation;

- **Birds** - there are several bird species in North America that are hunted for meat. Not all bird species are included on this list. Several smaller species are either too troublesome to bother hunting, or they embody a taste that is not considered flavorful
  - Dove
  - Partridge
  - Grouse
  - Pheasant
  - Ptarmigan
  - Quail
  - Turkey
  - Duck
  - Goose
- **Reptiles** - small game reptiles are another option to consider when hunting for survival. Several animals in this category can be harvested to make a meal. Certain reptiles may be poisonous and require special preparation before they can be consumed, so before hunting the animals listed here, it is highly

recommended you conduct regional research on the species in your area and know how to prepare them safely before you venture out looking for them

- o Frogs
- o Turtles
- o Snakes

➢ **Mammals** - there are several animals that could be included in this category; some of them larger than others, but they are not considered to be big game. In certain cases, a single animal from this group will be enough to feed a family of four or more; in other cases, you will need to harvest several animals of the same species to make a meal

- o Wild boar
- o Raccoon
- o Beaver
- o Muskrat
- o Squirrels
- o Rabbits
- o Hares
- o Opossums

Hunting Strategies

There are several strategies that can be employed when hunting that will make locating and taking a target animal easier to achieve. Remember that some of the strategies employ devices that may have restrictions within the state where the hunt takes place. In a life or death situation, those restrictions may be overlooked; taking an animal out of season while trying to survive being lost and stranded in the wilderness is unlikely to land you in jail. Hunting strategies to consider include, but are not limited to;

> **Baiting** - this strategy employs the use of anything that can attract a target animal, such as food, animal scents, decoys, and lures. The purpose of baiting is to bring a target animal to a specific area that is being monitored. The animal becomes distracted by the bait and the hunter has an easier time making a kill shot

> **Blind Hunting** - this does not refer to closing your eyes, but rather to the construction of a concealed hunting position. Blinds can be built on the ground, or they can be arranged at a higher elevation, such as in a tree

> **Calling** - normally employs the use of specialized equipment that recreates sounds the target animal is known to produce. An example of this would be duck and turkey calls. Calls are often used to attract animals to a given location, thus making the hunt easier on the hunter

> **Camouflaging** - is a strategy that is often used in combination with other strategies. It involves concealing yourself and your scent, allowing you to blend into the surrounding environment without alerting the target animals in the vicinity

> **Dogs** - these animals have been an instrumental part of hunting ever since they were domesticated. Dogs are used to flush, track, chase, and retrieve target animals,

> **Driving** - is a strategy that herds target animals in a specific direction, normally to a group of waiting hunters, but it can also involve herding target

animals to a known impasse, such as the edge of a cliff, or a boxed in canyon

➢ **Flushing** - is often done with dogs. The dogs are released and allowed to run after small game which scares the small game out of their hiding places, which gives the hunter a better opportunity at achieving a successful hunt

➢ Scouting—is a strategy that hunters use to determine if there are sufficient game animals in the area. Scouting is not the same as tracking. When a hunter scouts an area, they are looking for obvious signs that the area has the potential to support a variety of wildlife, such as a natural water source, ample food sources, etc.

➢ **Shining** - involves the use of artificial light to temporarily blind a target animal. This strategy is normally applied in low light conditions and freezes the animal in its tracks, thus making it easier for the hunter to take the animal

➢ **Stalking** - this strategy involves finding fresh animal signs which are then followed. The hunter hopes to sneak up on an animal and take it from a safe distance before the animal realizes it is being stalked

➢ **Tracking** - this is normally part of stalking, but it can also involve identifying heavily trafficked game trails which can then be used to devise a strategy for taking target animals from the area

➢ **Trapping** - this hunting strategy is normally employed to secure target animals without the need to monitor an area or deploy a different hunting strategy. Traps are often set on game trails and are designed to catch a specific type of target animal. Traps that are designed to catch a rabbit, more than likely will not work on a squirrel or a bird, and vice versa

Hunting with Weapons

Hunting for survival can take on many looks and strategies; it can also involve the use of several types of weapons. Firearms are an obvious choice when discussing the ability to hunt successfully; however, one should also consider the use of bows hunting systems, from long bows and compound box configurations to crossbows and slingshots, not to mention the use of spears and atlatls.

Rifles & Shotguns

While most people associate game hunting with rifles, when it comes to small game hunting, shotguns may provide a better solution and improve the chances of a successful hunt.

In order to hunt small game with a rifle, you generally want to use a small caliber, like a .22, which is just large enough to make the kill, but not so large it destroys most of the meat. The biggest challenge with using a rifle to hunt small game is that you have to be extremely accurate, and in most cases, you will need to be able to land a kill shot on a target animal that has been spooked into running.

When you hunt small game with a shotgun, this challenge is significantly reduced. Shotgun shells normally contain a significant number of projectiles, which when fired, create a spread pattern. This reduces the need for pinpoint accuracy which is necessary when hunting with a rifle that fires a single projectile down range and improves the chances of making a hit that will take the animal down.

Handguns for Hunting

While hunting with handguns is an option, there are several drawbacks to doing so in a survival situation. Handguns are lighter and more compact to carry, but they also lack accuracy over long distances.

In order to hunt successfully with a handgun, it generally has to incorporate a long barrel; the longer the barrel the further the round will travel with accuracy. Handguns are unable to shoot as far as rifles; the shorter barrel results in a rapid loss of velocity when the round exits the barrel. This causes the bullet to drop significantly, which results in the need to be much closer to the target animal when hunting. If you choose to hunt small game with a handgun, then the recommended caliber is again a .22 round.

Bows & Crossbows

Bows & Crossbows are another option to consider when hunting small land based animals. They are not the weapons of choice for hunting birds. Bows and crossbows may be lighter to carry than rifles and shotguns, however they may be a bit bulkier to bring along. Hunting with these types of weapons normally requires the hunter to be in fairly close proximity to the game animal being harvested; long distance shots are seldom accurate, effective, or efficient and if they do strike an animal it will normally result in a wound rather than a kill.

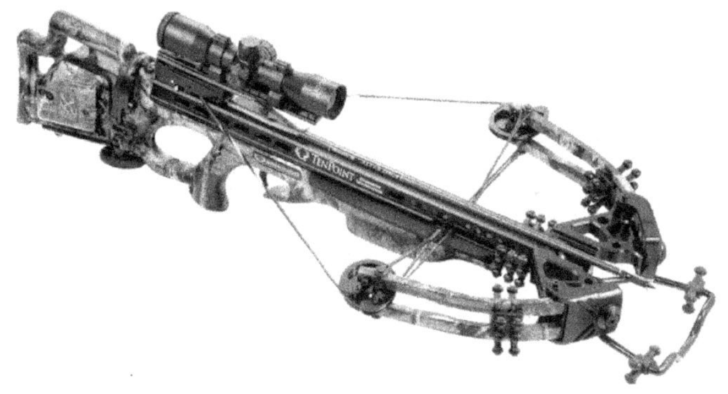

Bows & Crossbows are also generally used when hunting from a stationary position where target animals are lured into the kill zone, such as from a tree stand overlooking a bait pile or salt lick. While they can be used to stalk game animals, landing a kill shot on an animal that has been spooked into running with a bow/crossbow, requires a level of experience most novice hunters do not possess, and it also increases the risk of losing the arrow/bolt permanently.

Hunting Without Firearms

Hunting can also be done without the use of firearms, or with the limited use of firearms. The methods discussed here will allow the individual to hunt passively instead of actively. Rather than tracking, stalking, or hunting from a blind, these tactics allow the hunter to place gear and equipment in a targeted area where it can be left unattended and checked periodically. While a firearm is not necessarily used as the primary source for harvesting the animal, it may be necessary to use a firearm to finish the kill.

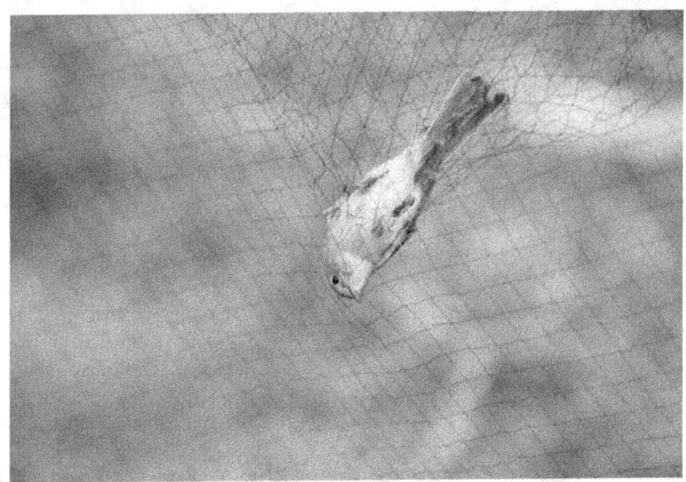

Trapping Techniques

The use of traps to harvest animals has been around for millennia. Historic evidence suggests that humans have been using animal traps since at least the earliest part of the Stone Age. Early civilizations used animal traps for many of the same reasons they are still used today; pest and varmint control, fur trading, food, and wildlife management.

There are several types of traps that can be used to harvest animals. The single biggest drawback to trapping animals is that the devices used for these methods do not always kill the animal humanely; it may be necessary to finish the job personally when a wounded animal is found in one of the traps. Below is a list of trapping techniques with brief descriptions for each. Again, readers are advised to seek the assistance of a local professional to provide them with instruction and guidance for trapping small game familiar to the region they live in;

> **Netting** - is one of the simplest forms of trapping small game. It is often reserved for trapping birds. Nets are arranged to hang between trees, or branches of trees, where birds are known to rest. The nets are difficult for the birds to see. As the bird flies into the net it becomes tangled and cannot escape. This often results in an injury to the bird, such as a broken wing, and/or a broken neck.
> **Deadfall Traps** - these are DIY designs that are created out of raw material found on location, such as a large rock or log, supported by smaller sticks and possibly even some cordage. The rock/log is placed at an angle over a game trail where it is

supported by smaller branches, one of which serves as the trigger for the trap; the trigger is often baited. When a target animal takes the bait, the trigger branch moves and causes the entire trap to fall suddenly, trapping the game animal beneath. There are several versions of the deadfall trap; figure four and Paiute to name a few, be sure to learn them all as they are fairly easy to setup in the wild.

➤ **Snares** - are devices that use cable/wire nooses to secure a game animal around the neck or body. They are generally placed on a game trail in such a way that allows target animals to try and pass through them. When a target animal trips a snare the noose closes around the animal. The more the animal struggles the tighter the noose closes.

➤ Trapping Pits - are DIY designs that basically consist of digging deep pits. The depth of the pit should be such that the animal falling into it cannot easily climb, jump, or hop its way out of it. Trapping pits can be as simple as a pit camouflaged with ground cover, or they can be arranged with kill spikes so that animals falling into them are impaled on the spikes.

Off Grid Cooking Options

Now that we've covered several aspects associated with hunting and fishing for survival, perhaps we should spend a little time going over the various off-grid cooking options that are out there. Some of these methods will be unconventional but familiar, whereas others will be unfamiliar and may require further guidance and instruction before they can be used effectively.

Off grid cooking options will almost always include the use of fire, which means safety should be an important component of the process. Not only is there a risk of personal injury, there is also the risk of damaging the food; place the food too close to the coals and it can dry out rather quickly, place it too far away from the coals and it may not cook thoroughly enough to be suitable for human consumption.

Remember, in a survival situation you will more than likely be preparing wild game for sustenance; this means you need to know how to prepare the game safely so that it doesn't cause anyone to get ill; food poisoning is not something you want to deal with when faced with a survival situation.

Campfires

This is the most common method of off-grid cooking. If you've ever operated a coal fired grill in the backyard before, then you have enough experience to cook over a campfire. You may need to fabricate a makeshift grill or use your imagination to heat rocks and use them as cooking pans, but you should be able to get the job done with relative ease.

Depending on the weather, campfires may be somewhat difficult to manage. High winds or shifting breezes can cause one side of the fire to cook faster than the others; it can also cause the ashes of the fire to contaminate the food. Rain can also be a restricting factor when trying to cook over the open flame of a campfire.

The use of additional equipment and gear will make cooking over a campfire easier to achieve. A makeshift spit placed over the center of the fire will keep food at the preferred height and allow the chef to rotate the meal with ease. A tripod can be arranged over a fire from which pots and kettles can be hung, and pans and grill grates will make the meal making process that much smoother.

Rocket Stoves

Rocket stoves can be constructed out of a wide variety of materials such as coffee and soup cans, or concrete blocks that are generally used in the construction of buildings. Rocket stoves incorporate a design that is engineered to funnel the heat from a fire through a condensed exhaust vent, thus making for a suitable place to cook food.

Rocket stoves do not require as much fuel as campfires. A handful of kindling and a small supply of dry twig sized branches are all that is normally required to get a rocket stove fired up and ready for cooking, which makes them very efficient devices for off grid cooking.

Underground Ovens

An underground oven is basically a luau pit. The pit is dug deep enough to house the meal and raw material from the surrounding area. The pit for the underground oven is also kept separate from the pit used to build a fire.

Once a fire has reduced to coals, the meal is prepped, which normally consists of wrapping it in a protective material such as aluminum foil or greenery from the surrounding area; palm leaves, elephant ear plants, etc. A bed of coal is placed in the bottom of the underground oven pit, the wrapped food is placed atop the bed of coals, and then the wrapped food is covered with another layer of coals, which is then covered with sand or earth.

Depending on the meal being cooked in the underground pit, it may be necessary to unearth it periodically to inspect the food for doneness. If the food is cooked thoroughly it should be removed, if not then it may need to be flipped and recovered with a fresh layer of coals and earth.

Dutch Ovens

Dutch Ovens can be used to bake breads, pies, cobblers, cakes, casseroles, stews, etc. They are very easy to use and are only limited by their size. You can place a Dutch Oven on top of a bed of coals or dig a shallow trench and bury the Dutch Oven beneath a bed of coals.

Dutch Ovens are made out of cast iron which retains an immense amount of heat from a fire/coals, so they must be handled carefully when being removed to prevent the possibility of personal injury.

Solar Ovens

While there are several DIY cardboard and aluminum

foil designs, a manufactured solar oven will work far better than anything created on the fly.

Solar ovens magnify and redirect the rays of the sun to produce the heat required to cook food. The biggest drawback to cooking with a solar oven may be the size of the oven itself. Solar ovens are not industrious models like those found in traditional American kitchens, they are much smaller, which means they may not be big enough to prepare a whole meal simultaneously.

The upside of solar ovens is that the only thing required to make them work is a bright sun shiny day. There is no need to build a fire, nor is a special fuel required to make a solar oven function. You simply arrange the meal to be cooked, place it inside and check it periodically until it is done and ready to eat.

Additional Options

There is no shortage of off-grid cooking equipment to choose from. Hobo stoves, Sterno stoves, and Alcohol stoves are available in various configurations from a number of manufacturers and distributors.

It would be wise to have several options available and to have the knowledge and experience to use them efficiently, effectively, and safely. Consumption of raw food in a wilderness environment, especially the carcass of an animal, is not recommended despite survival stories to the contrary and should only be considered under the direst of circumstances.

DISCLAIMER AND/OR LEGAL NOTICES: Every effort has been made to accurately represent this book and it's potential. Results vary with every individual, and your results may or may not be different from those depicted. No promises, guarantees or warranties, whether stated or implied, have been made that you will produce any specific result from this book. Your efforts are individual and unique, and may vary from those shown. Your success depends on your efforts, background and motivation. The material in this publication is provided for educational and informational purposes only. Use of the programs, advice, and information contained in this book is at the sole discretion and risk of the reader

www.ingramcontent.com/pod-product-compliance
Lightning Source LLC
Chambersburg PA
CBHW061731250726
48657CB00002B/872